MY DAUGHTER KEEPS OUR HAMMER

Brian Watkins

I0139970

BROADWAY PLAY PUBLISHING INC
224 E 62nd St, NY, NY 10065
www.broadwayplaypub.com
info@broadwayplaypub.com

First printing: March 2015
I S B N: 978-0-88145-625-7

Book design: Marie Donovan
Page make-up: Adobe Indesign
Typeface: Palatino
Printed and bound in the U S A

MY DAUGHTER KEEPS OUR HAMMER was developed at b. swibel presents, an affiliate of Playing Pretend Productions (B. Swibel and Tara Smith, Artistic Directors; Stephanie Cowan, Director of Development; Adam Westbrook, Associate Artistic Director) between 2010-2013.

The play had its world premiere at The Flea Theater (Jim Simpson, Artistic Director; Carol Ostrow, Producing Director); the first performance was on 15 January 2014, the opening was on 25 January 2014. The cast and creative contributors were:

SARAH..Katherine Folk-Sullivan
HANNAH ....Layla Khoshnoudi

understudies:

SARAH.. Hannah Finn
HANNAH ....Kate Thulin

Director.. Danya Taymor
Set designer..Andrew Diaz
Lighting designer... John Eckert
Costume designer......................................Beth Goldenberg
Sound designer.. Adriano Shaplin
Stage manager.. Jasmine Olson

CHARACTERS & SETTING

SARAH, *older sister. 20s. Strong. Dutiful, hardworking, smart, a perfectionist. Bigger than her sister.*

HANNAH, *younger sister. 20's. Small. Ornery. Rebellious. A waitress and a total firecracker.*

Time: The recurring past

A NOTE ON THE STAGING

As the women deliver their story, the peripheral action should suggest their memories coming to life, the past becoming present. The women speak directly to the audience. No attempt at a naturalistic "fourth wall" need be made. These are fictional characters and real actors all at once. What's important in the playing is that it's happening in the immediate Now: the dramatic event is in the actual telling of their story. However, for those that might want some further context:

I've always felt that these women are delivering their story in a purgatorial setting, not dissimilar to the plains on which their story takes place, nor dissimilar to an empty stage in a dark theater. With that, one might consider that the women are speaking to an authority. What authority someone in a sort of purgatory might be speaking to can be left to the imagination. The women's objective, then, could be to be heard, hoping that in being heard, they might be freed.

Lastly, any attempt at an eastern Coloradoan dialect is welcomed, but not essential. More important is that these women are strong, rural Americans.

If I ask you, angel, will you come and lead
This ache to speech, or carry me, like a child,
To riot?

—Edgar Bowers, *Autumn Shade*

Ho, wind from the western prairies
Ho, voice from a far domain
I feel in your breath what I'll feel till death,
The call of the plains again.

—American folk song

PROLOGUE

(Silence in complete, pitch black before SARAH *enters and delivers the following in total dark.)*

SARAH: O K…alright.
Well if I have to do this I just wanna say that…some 'a these things…are outta' my control…alright?
(Beat)
When I was a kid my Mom told me this story 'bout my great grandma—from my Mom's side, the Peterson side. Her generation was the first to homestead in Eaton, a hundred-some years ago.
And they were there during the blizzard of 1880. To make things worse, the summer before there'd been this drought that killed all their crops.
So after the drought, they had set up these community refuges. And you would hike out to this refuge to collect food and supplies to bring back to your family. And they'd do this every week or so, to survive the whole winter.
So one day my great grandma hikes out to this refuge to pick up the food.
And the way you spotted the refuge…was by this lantern.

(We hear someone strike a match 3 times. It flares up and burns, illuminating the hand of the fire bearer, producing a faint orange glow upstage, far away from SARAH.*)*

SARAH: An' they'd always keep the lantern lit, so folks could see where they ought to go.
So she set out for this refuge. Eight miles away.
Trekkin' out across the plains.
And she gets a few miles out there…and the blizzard hits. Can't see a thing.
But she keeps goin'. Keeps trekkin' on. Through all that snow, all that white. Lookin' for that lantern, lookin' for that light. Tryin' to get somewhere.
But she never got anywhere… She never saw the lantern.

(The orange glow from the match flickers out.)

SARAH: They figured she'd died out there. Frozen to death. But they never found a body.

(Pause)

So then my Mom told me that there was some speculation 'round what happened to her: that maybe she got picked up or captured, or maybe the coyotes got to her…or that maybe she was still out there.
And my Mom's tellin' me all this—I must've been seven or eight—and I'm just tremblin'…scared outta' my wits. Cuz, ya know, as a kid I really, truly thought there was a chance that my great grandma was still out there.
So every once and a while…I'd light this candle and put it in my window, as a light for my great grandma to see, in case she was still out there.

(We hear a match struck 3 times before it flares up and lights. The hand of the fire-bearer takes the match and lights a candle.)

SARAH: And one night…I was layin' awake in bed… and I heard some noise out on the prairie. Like someone callin' out.

I looked out my window…and saw this woman off in the distance on the plains comin' towards me. In like ragged clothes, carryin' some sort of basket.

Her arm was outstretched towards my window. Like she was drawn to the flame.

I watched her get closer and closer and eventually just got so afraid that I blew that candle out right quick…

(The fire-bearer blows out the flame.)

SARAH: …and just laid back down in bed, hopin' that woman wouldn't come any closer.

I ran into my Mom's room and told her what I saw, just terrified…and she laughed at me. She said "I knew that story would spook you." Told me I was just dreaming…sent me back to bed…laughin' at me as I walked away.

And I kinda hated her right then.

Cuz why would she go and tell me that? I didn't need to know that, ya know?

Some things oughtn't be passed down.

(Beat)

So. I just thought I should prolly tell you that…if I have to tell you this.

(Silence. Darkness)

END OF PROLOGUE

PART 1

(Lights blast on to reveal HANNAH *stage left,* SARAH *stage right. Both standing. Far upstage, the remnants of a recent fire are very dimly lit. The pile consists of some ash, a few cinders, and a number of charred logs. Part of* SARAH's *shirt and arms are covered in soot. Both girls' clothes are ragged and dusty and worn out, yet their composure is far from reflecting any ounce of exhaustion.)*

HANNAH: Me and my sister don't talk.

SARAH: Hannah and I don't talk much.

HANNAH: We never talk.

SARAH: She's very independent.

HANNAH: Sarah will never tell you *why* we don't, but I'll say it: Mom.

SARAH: Over time, things happen.

HANNAH: Ever since our Mom's been shut in, we just stopped talking.

SARAH: Some families just don't talk much. Isn't that ok?

(Beat. HANNAH *looks to the sky.)*

SARAH: But when we do it's usually when Hannah's tryin' to get out of somethin'.
She's a true native in that sense: Everyone here is tryin' to get out.

HANNAH: Eaton isn't far from some other bigger towns, but that doesn't make it not small, it's small. For Colorado.

By car you're lookin' at only ten minutes from Greeley but you'd think it was hours from civilization seein' all the space we came upon.

Now it's mostly empty ranches, cuz of all the new factories.

No one's got any reason to keep a ranch or a farm anymore. You live in Eaton, you better get keen to that quick: *That's* all over.

The fact they haven't turned all that land into a bunch a' cookie-cutter houses is a miracle to me.

If we got a mall I wouldn't mind that but I think I'd get lost if they built one a' those subdivisions all the homes look alike. I'd be knockin' on a different house every day tryin' to find my own place.

SARAH: You come into town you'll be comin' on a highway runnin' up into Wyoming thru Ault and thru Pierce and thru those ugly lookin' pasture towns 'fore you hit the border and then you got Cheyenne…

So headin' north you got plains on your right and then mountains on your left, but they're a far ways off yet. You can't see 'em 'less you're really lookin' for em'.

I forget they're even there sometimes.

HANNAH: The restaurant I'm at sits right on the highway there but looks out across the prairie to the east.

I open most mornings 'round five A M while it's still dark outside.

I usually spend a good hour just starin' out across that prairie as the dawn breaks from the east, when there's just a few fucknuts drinkin' coffee in there and *gawd*: it's just the same folks each and every day.

SARAH: I'm cooped up at home mostly, so it'd be nice to see folks more often…

HANNAH: And I guess some people might enjoy that…

SARAH: That'd be nice. I'd like that.

HANNAH: …but I just kinda hate it. That aspect.
It's mostly truckers and ranchers come in talkin' to me.
Givin' me nicknames or what not.
"Hannah Honey." "Short Stack Hannah." Ya know, fuckin' pancakes or whatever.
The nicknames I can deal with, but it's just people knowin' me and knowin' 'bout my family or whatever that gets on my nerves.
I'll do anything to get a guy to shutup.
(She goes and grabs a twine-bound stack of newspapers.)

SARAH: I don't really have a job right now. Don't have the time.
Wish I had the time, but my Mom's become a full time gig is the way I think of it.
I'm always runnin' errands or cleanin' the house or somethin'. Which is fine.
It's just a hell of a lot of chores, I guess…
But I don't mind.
I grew up doin' 'em and so chores were somethin' we've always done because there were always chores to do and so that's what you did.
So that's what I still do.
And I guess I'm just used to it. Second nature.
If I ain't got a chore to do I feel sort of out of whack, ya know…
Don't really know what to do with myself.
That's just what I learned.
An' some people say that's what makes me anal-retentive or whatever but I always said its better'n bein' idle.

Devil's workshop and all that…
So I'm better off without a job…considerin' the laundry
list of tasks it is keepin' the house goin'.
I coulda' gone to college. I had the grades. I did, really.
But when duty calls…

(HANNAH *places the newspapers in front of the pile of ash
upstage.*)

SARAH: You can only know so many people in this
town, so it goes without sayin' that you can only go to
high school with so few less of 'em.
I graduated with twenty-two of 'em and as sayin' goes
they all seemed bound for shit or a shotgun weddin' so
I'm just happy to be without a divorce at this point.
This town is quiet for the most part, until you get a
domestic dispute goin', but even then still…
Even if you're *screamin'* at someone seems like who
cares there's no one else can hear it.
Which gives rise to the question of talkin' at all.
(Like: right here. Like: here ya go.)
So whatever problem you got's just bound to swallow
itself in the silence.
Right?
(To the heavens, bashfully:)
Hello?
(Silence. She nods her head, trying to go on.)
So me and my sister, I think we're better off livin' with
Mom right now anyway.
But I guess we might have different opinions on that.

HANNAH: My Dad's not around anymore.
Just me and my sister and my Mom.
I'm usually gone. Sarah's usually home. With Mom.
We got a good amount of land but only a tiny house.
When my Dad got the house, back whenever, I guess
he didn't wanna spend too much money on a big place.

Spent most of his money on his truck.

Which we still got.

The truck I mean.

It's a '85 Ford F-150 and it's sittin' in the damn garage
with nothin' but a clean coat of wax and a little dust on
it.

It's in mint condition. Hasn't been driven since he was
here.

He cared for that truck more than he cared for us an'
my Mom always said that's why I'm so short. Said
my Dad spent more money waxin' that thing up than
buyin' us proper vegetables to eat and as a result I've
got a stunted growth.

I don't blame him though. It's a sweet ass truck.

SARAH: I've had a plan for a while now to go to school.
I was thinkin' that if my Mom ever gave me that
truck—that's just sittin' out there in the garage—then
maybe ya know that might be a start.

I could sell *it* and use the money for tuition or
whatever.

I'd like that.

But the keys to that truck ain't gettin' pried from
Mom's hands any time soon.

She's actually got 'em locked up…in a, like a, jewelry
case in her bedroom 'cuz she knows Hannah'd beg,
borrow, and steal to get that damn thing.

She's drivin' an Isuzu-piece-a-crap right now that's on
its last leg, so…

(She exits.)

HANNAH: I got this Isuzu piece-of-horse-shit-disabled-
damn-thing with about half a million miles on it and in
the winter it's like drivin' a damn igloo around 'cuz the
damn heater doesn't work.

The thing breaks down if you take it above forty!

And I'll tell ya: I've done the math. Guess, on average, how many miles your ass can drive this thing 'til it's overheated.

Thirty-seven. Thirty-seven miles. It's like the car has one 'a those fuckin' electric dog collars on it, shocks 'em if they wander outside the yard.

You take that thing outside Weld County and it's like boom: "Fuck you! I'm breakin' down!"

So I'm stuck.

And I'm thinkin': c'mon, there's a fresh truck sittin' in our garage an' our Mom don't want anybody drivin' it because of sentimental value?

(SARAH *enters, carrying a load of twigs and branches and pine needles. She puts it down in front of the pile of ash upstage.*)

HANNAH: Here I am on the verge of pneumonia every time I climb into this death trap, and she's carin' more about keepin' memories.

Ya know, it's a wonder that me and my sister haven't up and left that woman, considerin' all that we've done for her.

I'm not sure why the hell each of us care anymore, she's on her last leg anyway, so it's just a matter of time, but still, here *we* are, takin' her to the doctor, pickin' up her meds...

(*Beat*)

I should've told you: She's sick...

SARAH: Our Mom is sick.

HANNAH: ...It's somethin' is wrong with her bones or somethin'...

SARAH: She's got this arthritis, keeps her from movin' much...

HANNAH: Somewhat better for me and my sister, seein'
as she's not wanderin' around all over the house,
gettin' into trouble in the storage space or wherever.

SARAH: We've got this nice little area set up for her in
front of the T V next to the window so she spends most
of her days there.

HANNAH: Sarah takes care of her. Bein' older and more
responsible and more of a kiss ass an' all that.

SARAH: Hannah's usually at work or out or God knows
where so I'm always pickin' up her medicine, makin'
sure she's takin' the right pills, makin' sure the TV isn't
too loud.
Her hearin' is kinda shot, so she's usually got that
thing just blastin'.
She's been catchin' those Hollywood celebrity shows
recently. Keeps yappin' at me tellin' me 'bout which
movie star is datin' who and then how they're all just a
bunch of hussies anyway, so…
I try an' make sure she doesn't have it stuck on those
channels.
I don't know how on earth she got cable.

HANNAH: I rigged the place with cable so that I
wouldn't be bored as shit when I'm at home. I know a
guy. He took care of it.

SARAH: She said one day the channels just popped up.

HANNAH: An' the bill ain't in my name so, ya know, no
one's gettin' hurt here.
I always said: what you don't know won't hurt you.
And I think that's pretty much a failsafe philosophy.
(She goes and grabs kindling.)

SARAH: So there's plenty to do for my Mom, ya know,
whatever, I don't like it but it's got to be done: makin'
sure she's eatin', takin' her meds, all that.

I got to take her down to the hospital every once and a while. I got to clean her.

(Beat)

But what I'm doin' mostly is takin' care of her sheep.

(Beat. She nervously fixes her hair.)

There's only one of 'em. We used to have some thirty or forty head of 'em when my Dad was around but we got rid of most of 'em to pay for medical bills or…pay for groceries or whatever else.

And, ya know, tendin' a sheep is not like tendin' a dog or a cat.

There's nothin' that the damn thing gives back to you, although Mom'd argue otherwise.

So unless you're in the goddamn sweater business there ain't any reason to expect anything but chores from a damn sheep.

'Course you gotta keep it watered and fed, but first you gotta measure the hay.

Keep it up high so they don't piss or poop on it.

You gotta fan the stall. Sawdust the stall.

Check its hooves. Clean its hooves. Trim its hooves.

Check for scours. Clean the crap that gets stuck on its back end.

Crutch the anus. Crutch the teats. Trim the fleece around the eyes.

And on top 'a that you're muckin' its stall 'bout once a week.

(HANNAH enters with an armful of kindling. She plops it down upstage near the pile of ash. Then, she does it again.)

SARAH: It's kinda funny: we've got stables out back where there's enough room for maybe fifty animals but it's just the one out there, fartin' around like a dumbass sheep.

Just standin' there.

So after a while Mom started feelin' bad 'cuz the thing was always alone.

But she wanted to see it and bein' sick and stuff she couldn't quite get out to the pens to have a look, ya know.

So of course then it's got to come in the house.

So I started bringin' it inside for her during the day like a…companion or whatever.

Like a nice little play date…somethin' to look forward to each day.

It always goes a little nuts when it's in there, ya know, 'cuz its a goddamn sheep, a *wild* animal…

She named the sheep Vicky.

I'm not sure if there's any background on that other than she thought Vicky'd be a good name for a sheep. But that's its name. Vicky.

(Beat)

And the reason Vicky outlasted the other animals was because Vicky was special.

Vicky was a gift.

My Dad bought her for my Mom on their twentieth anniversary.

And you gotta ask yourself, ya know, who the hell gives a sheep as a gift?

But I guess it's what she wanted 'cuz it sure made her happy when she got it and it has ever since.

(Beat)

So anyway, I let her have that sheep in the house and there was some cause for concern, ya know, 'cuz that's a damn dirty animal to keep inside.

That thing gets worms or whatever you got a big problem on your hands, sittin' in the livin' room…ya know?

(HANNAH brings on her final load of kindling, plops it down near the ash, and comes downstage.)

SARAH: But I let her have the thing inside during the day. Make her happy.

And you can't really keep someone from that... Can you?

HANNAH: Vicky's always been just a little bitch of a sheep and her main problem was that she was sneaky.

One day I come home from work and I guess Sarah told Mom she could have the thing in the house—why, I have no idea—but Sarah hadn't told me this.

And so I come in the house, and I shut the door behind me...and it's just standin' there behind the door! Starin' me down.

Like she'd been waitin' for me or somethin'. Scared the hell outta' me.

Those things are so skittish too, (ya know). Like you make one little move towards it and it'll freak out and sprint across the room.

So I yelped, and BANG, Vicky darts off like a madman.

So I never knew if Vicky was in the house or not until I'd walk into the kitchen and the damn thing would run into the livin' room and slam into the china cabinet or somethin' and Mom'd start yellin' at me, "Don't scare Vicky, goddamit!"

And there's nothin' you can do!

You got a piece 'a livestock runnin' renegade through your house!

And you can't housebreak those things. I don't care how much you try, when you got a brain the size of a pea...! Christ.

An' ya know, when I was little we had a bunch of 'em but I never tended to 'em—I was too young—so I don't really have much of a...idea of how to take care of 'em.

(SARAH *goes to the newspapers and takes some of them apart, setting them on the floor by the kindling and ash.*)

HANNAH: I used to watch my Dad sheer 'em…an' I remember that, but I…I don't think I remember much else.

But Mom especially loved Vicky. I mean she really…

Ya know it's a strange thing when you get someone lovin' somethin' you got no idea how they could love. Ya know?

I don't know how or why she cared so much for that damn sheep.

She remembers us havin' those things when we were kids…

…and she remembers our Dad—he took care of the place and all the animals.

I think she just wants to keep the last bit of what's left of that.

So we got a goddamn sheep in the house.

If I said that wasn't frustrating I'd be lying.

But like I was sayin'…sometimes you hate the things your family loves and I don't think that's totally uncommon.

So you try and fix it before it becomes, whatever, ya know, before it boils over.

But my Dad always used to say that you can't stop somethin' that's comin'.

It'll be here soon enough.

(SARAH *comes downstage.*)

SARAH: For some reason Vicky wasn't as fussy with my Mom as she was with me and Hannah.

She'd have the thing inside for a few hours and then I'd take it outside at night so it could sleep and eat where it naturally knows to.

An' so I'd take it out there around six or seven in the evening. Feed it. Shut it in.

And there was umm…this is weird.

I'm sorry, but this is just weird sayin' this, but uhh…
but I guess it's worth mentionin' if I'm to say…
(*Nervous chuckle, before:*)
O K.
One time, this was like six months ago…I was umm…I
was takin' Vicky out to the stables.
And ya know, the thing always fights you when you
bring it some place, and that's kinda annoying, ya
know, but whatever: it's a sheep.
So it's sort of bein' unruly and it's really pissin' me off
and so I'm draggin' it to its pen and I'm grittin' my
teeth talkin' to it and I'm sayin: Yeah Vicky, you wanna
fight me?
An' I've got this real mean look on my face and so I
sort of wrangle it into the pen and toss some hay at it
and I head back towards the house.
But then…outta' nowhere, I don't know why…I had
gotten almost all the way back to the house…
But then I stopped.
And I turned around and started back towards the pen.
And I went into the pen and I squeezed Vicky's face
with my hand and I just started slappin' her across the
mouth.
Over and over again, just slappin' her with my open
hand.
(*Beat*)
An' I know that's messed up…but I just…I dunno.
There was somethin' in me that…
Ya know, so I stood there and I slapped her a few times
and then umm…then I uhhh…well, I spit on her.
(*She holds her breath with an awkward smile.*)
I'm not sure if Vicky knew what was goin' on or
anything it just looked bewildered and stupid as usual.
But still I sort of caught myself off guard there. Shook
me up a little.

I wouldn't ever tell my Mom that I did that but I did it.
So I guess, ya know…take that for what you will.
(She looks off, embarrassed.)
I went back inside. An' I guess I just felt bad about…
what I'd done. So I umm…
I'd been workin' on this quilt that my Mom was doin'
but she had to stop doin' 'cuz of her fingers and all…
and she was always askin' me to finish it for her.
I had never, just, ya know, I'd never gotten around to
it. I was gonna do it. But…
It was this quilt with sorta' like a family tree thing on
it.
It had all these names on the outside of it that I never
heard of.
And she had all the squares chronologically connected
and, ya know, it was brown. And the names were in
green. Green and brown.
And the…center square 'a that quilt…had this
embroidery on it, this quote or whatever, that was so
stupid it just stuck in my brain.
It said: "May our mothers keep us healthy, may our
daughters keep us proud… May our sisters keep us
happy, and our family remember how."
Except "remember" was spelled with a "d".
And so it said "rememder", like someone had screwed
it up or somethin'.
Like someone didn't "rememder" how to spell.
Which made me think that some idiot prolly just read
that quote at some craft show and tried to put it on a
quilt but was too stupid to get it right.
Bunch 'a ladies 'round here do that kinda crap.
Crafts or whatever.
But as far as this quilt goes they're not very good at it.
So anyway I'm lookin' at this unfinished quilt and
there's this stupid mistake right smack in the middle of

it, and I'm thinkin': if you're gonna do somethin' do it right, ya know!

So I never got around to piecing that quilt together for Mom until that night...

(Vehemently, through her teeth:)

And I finished the fucker.

(Clears her throat, before:)

(Sorry.)

That's the fastest I ever seen my hands work, I'll tell you that, but it was like I just got to doin' somethin' and it just...came to me.

And as I was doin' it I was seein' all these names: Peterson, Sullivan, Henry...

And it was strange, I had these memories 'a these people I never knew...

I started...makin' up these stories in my mind 'bout what they done...who they were...these strangers.

Thinkin' they'd done the same things, seen the same places...

When I was done I went out and showed it to my Mom.

I seen her smile for one quick second and I could tell that she was surprised but then just as quick I seen her tighten her lips and she said: Well it's about time.

I told her I was sorry it took me so long.

She said she was too.

She told me where I messed up on some of the stitching.

She said: I thought I'd die before that quilt got finished.

I thought of something to say back to her...but I didn't.

It was just a stupid quilt. But I did it. And that's what counts.

That's what counts.

(Beat)

Hannah wasn't home then but I told her about it later.

(SARAH *goes off stage and brings on a number of twigs and sticks and plops them upstage.*)

HANNAH: Next day Mom was ravin' 'bout this damn quilt that Sarah finished for her outta' the blue. And she's yappin' all 'bout how much more Sarah loved her than I did and how she was always around and takin' care of Vicky and what did I ever do for her, my mother, the woman who brought me into this world and blah blah blah...

And, ya know, I'm just kinda like: yeah, whatever, ok.

But then she got my attention.

I'm walkin' away from her as she's watchin' her damn Entertainment Tonight, and she says: ya know, I'm inclined to give Sarah your Dad's old truck for all the nice things she's been doin' for me lately.

(Beat)

And I stopped.

And I said...*what*?

An' she says: I might give her the truck. As a surprise. Yep. I think I might. For Christmas maybe.

An' I'm thinkin': well shit.

I been waitin' to get that truck for as long as I can remember and now after one shitty little blanket all of a sudden Sarah's got it?

I never thought my Mom would hand that thing over to either of us.

Thought I'd have to pry the keys out of her dead hands.

(SARAH *exits again and brings back on an armful of firewood and sorts through each piece, methodically separating each log by shape and size.*)

HANNAH: So I'm in bed that night thinkin', shit, ya know, I got until Christmas to one up her here.

An' I'm thinkin': what the hell can I do to commandeer that damn F-150?

I'm off to work the next mornin', tossin' plates of
eggs and bacon to the regulars and the early mornin'
truckers…

And they're all yappin' my ear off 'bout some burrito-
sellin' billboard model they were all droolin' over on
their drive from Sioux Falls to Denver or somethin'
(I dunno, I came in on the end of what they were
sayin'…)

An' I'm at this one guys table—he ranches over in
Pierce I think—and I hear him talkin' 'bout this new
ram he's off to pick up in Laramie.

And it dawns on me: Here's an opportunity.

Now, you're gonna think I'm nuts for thinkin' this but
if you were from Eaton you'd call me a genius.

So I say to this guy, I said: You got a ram?

He says: Yeah.

An' ya know, I'm not much of a farm girl. Like I said,
we did that shit when I was little but I never really
paid attention, so I'm not totally sure how all that
works.

So I say to this guy: Rams, they have sex with sheep,
right?

An' he looks at me in sort of a pervert way and says:
You bet they do, honey.

An' I say: You lookin' to breed that ram?

An' he says: Well I ain't gonna try an' milk it. (Fuckin'
smart ass, right?)

So I tell him: hey, I'll give you fifty bucks if you get
your ram to have sex with my sheep.

An' he's lookin' at me like I'm a little crazy but then
I tell him: well, ya know…I wanna get the sheep
pregnant.

An' he says: just one sheep?

An' I say: yeah.

'Cuz lets be realistic here. Vicky's not gonna be alive forever. An' I guess you could say that Mom isn't either, but look: there's one thing Mom would love even more than Vicky, and that's two Vickys.

I can just see it: One day after that damn thing is bleatin' and pushin' that little lamb out its back end I bring it inside with a bottle full a' two percent and put it in my Mom's arms…

That'd blow her damn mind.

An' all of a sudden: Here ya go Hannah, here's a nice ass truck for you to do with whatever you like…

As much as I'd hate two 'a those damn animals runnin' round the house I'd love a nice shiny F-150 even more.

Drive my ass outta' there.

Head down to San Diego or some place.

Maybe see the ocean.

Get off the plains.

(Beat)

So here we go, ya know: I'm all happy an' stuff 'cuz I got this great plan, and shit this is just brilliant.

Crazy. But brilliant.

(SARAH goes off and comes back with more wood, repeating her task of sorting, ever so methodically.)

HANNAH: So I get this rancher over to our place one day while Mom and Sarah were gone.

They went to the doctor to have Mom take some tests or whatever, so I knew I had a good three or four hours to get Vicky pregnant.

And of course I didn't tell Sarah 'bout my grand plan here because, ya know, the whole thing is dependent on the element-of-surprise-deal.

Guy comes over with this Mexican dude he brought with him to help him out.

We get there an' he just pulls his ram out the back of his trailer and it's buckin' an' goin' a little crazy, so

he and his guy there just kinda grab it on either side
its head an they pull it out, toss it in the pen, and then
immediately run away from it. Like rodeo clowns
tauntin' a bull.

Then they go and they grab Vicky.

An they done this a million times, so it feels like some
childhood memory come alive in front of me they were
so familiar with what they were doin'.

But it was maybe a little weird.

We set there with Vicky and the ram in the same area
waitin' for the ram to make its move.

And I guess this guy had some method where he'd talk
to the ram, and encourage it and what not. So he starts
makin' these sounds like "hep hep" "go on it" "there
yar" "get up on 'er" "get up on 'er there"…

An' I'm just watchin' him thinkin': I've hired me a
fuckin' nut case.

Either that or one a' those crazy-ass animal whisperers
but they aren't so different from a nut case anyway.

It was so weird lookin' 'cuz the ram starts doin' this
thing where it starts pawin' the ground with its front
hoof which is what I guess they do when they're gettin'
ready for it…

And the ram stands up close to Vicky and is doin' this
thing with its leg and makin' weird noises and stuff
and it's all really interesting but it feels like we maybe
shouldn't be watchin' this, ya know…

Like we maybe should give 'em some privacy or
somethin'.

But it's like a car wreck, ya know, you can't help but
look at that. I just can't take my eyes off the whole
mess…

And the guys are still yellin' at it and we're all
mesmerized by watching this ram just hop up on the
back of this sheep.

So I ask the guy: What's the chances this right here gets
her pregnant?
And he says: well, how old is she?
And I think back on it…how long we had Vicky…ten
years. At least ten years.
The guy says: are you kiddin' me? The chance of gettin'
this sheep pregnant is about one in a hundred.
One in a hundred? One in a hundred?! Are you kiddin'
me?
Christ, when I was in high school they were tellin' me
I could get pregnant even through a dude's pants and
now you're tellin' me that after watchin' that horrific
thing that Vicky's got—sonofabitch!
Jesus. That's a waste of fifty bucks.
So now I'm kinda pissed off thinkin' what the hell, ya
know.
But it's still like I couldn't help but watch those things
go at it, angry as I was.
And the ram's givin' it to her for a good long while
now and Vicky's kinda shiverin' and all wrinkled up
lookin' like an embarrassed grandma or somethin'.
And we just set there.
Watchin 'em have sex.
(Pause)
And that's how I spent my Wednesday afternoon.

(Pause)

*(SARAH stops and dusts off her hands and examines her
work.)*

END OF PART 1

PART 2

(Sound and lights quickly shift.)

SARAH: There's some people can't get enough 'a their own birthday and our Mom is one of 'em.

So like five months later, when her sixtieth birthday rolled around, she made sure that we'd remember the thing like it was the goddamn second coming.

It's like the whole week leadin' up to it she just can't help but talk 'bout it.

Which is fine, that's fine, (I guess it's fine), but it gets to a point where you're thinkin': ...well what about me? Check me out, ya know?!

Here I am, slavin' over the whole house...

When my birthday rolls around there ain't a peep until day of.

So don't go yappin' at me *ten days out* that you wanna go to Chilis for your birthday dinner!

That's fine. But last time I checked, they don't take reservations!

So just sit tight, ya know? It's on the goddamn calendar!

And I shoulda' known better that she'd have a change of heart when the big day finally came along.

So I played nice when she told me that she'd rather have me make her dinner at home, but truth be told I was just boilin' inside.

HANNAH: So I get off work, come home, and we gotta celebrate Mom's birthday or whatever and Sarah says: hey, Mom's not feelin' so hot. We're stayin' in. Makin' her dinner.

And I'm thinkin': shit man, I was lookin' forward to goin' to Chili's or some place and now I'm cooped up here for the whole night, with a sick old lady, a kiss ass, and a sheep.

SARAH: I asked her what she wanted for dinner and for some reason she said she wanted chicken parmesan. And I'm thinkin': what? When did you start likin' chicken parmesan? Mom, I never even seen you eat chicken parmesan! Seriously?!

And she goes off into some story about she had it once on a date with our dad and how she's always liked it, and I'm thinkin': Christ. This lady isn't gonna shut up until she gets some chicken parmesan.

HANNAH: So me and Sarah drive out to the store, pickin' up ingredients for chicken-fuckin-parmesan. And this is a goddamn labor-intensive meal, ya know? This ain't like a damn casserole or whatever, you can't just toss it together. We gotta do all this shit that just seems a little excessive.

Recipe is sayin' to make these breadcrumbs, make some sorta' batter, flatten the chicken, boil this, simmer that.

C'mon!

And I turn to Sarah sayin': Can you believe this? We're bustin' our ass to make her somethin' we didn't even know she liked and so what the fuck?

But Sarah just stands there. Smilin'. Smilin': bullshit. I can see right through *that*.

I can see right through to that part 'a her that's mad as a hornet.

But she's grinnin' like a circus clown nonetheless.

I know she ain't happy.

I know she doesn't wanna do what she does but she does it 'cuz maybe she's so used to it that she just forgot…

Or maybe she's just nutso.

Or maybe she's afraid.

(Beat. She thinks.)

She had pretty bad acne in high school so I wonder if maybe that developed into some like self-image problem or somethin'. Some psychological disorder. If that's the case then a fuckin' dermatologist coulda' saved us a lot 'a trouble, I'll tell ya that.

SARAH: So we get to makin' this dinner and there's all this to do for the recipe and so I give Hannah the job of preparin' the chicken but she won't stop gripin' 'bout all the work we gotta do.

So she's flattenin' the chicken with one 'a those meat tenderizers and I'm simmerin' the sauce and preparin' the pasta, sorta' gettin' our hands dirty or whatever.

Mom's in the living room. Watchin' T V.

So Hannah's yappin' away and she goes off onto askin' me about "do I remember the time when Dad hired a *magician* for my birthday"…back when I was like eight or nine.

And I said: yeah, I remember.

And she goes off on rememberin' how the guy was a really bad magician and how Mom thought he was drunk…

And she was right, he was this weird guy. This magician.

I remember he was missin' a finger or somethin'.

Which is kinda messed up for a magician, ya know, 'cuz you're starin' at his hands most 'a the time anyway.

And you start thinkin': how the hell did this magician
lose his finger.

Maybe it was just somethin' really normal like he got
a really bad paper cut from one of the cards and it got
infected or somethin' and eventually they just had to
cut it off.

Or maybe he was doin' that trick where it looks like
you're takin' your finger off but you're actually not but
maybe somethin' went wrong one time and somehow
the magic actually worked.

And off his finger came.

And the kids start freakin' out and he starts freakin'
out and there's blood…

'Cuz you gotta think: someone does *real* magic…well
that's just terrifying.

I remember Hannah and me were sittin' cross-legged
in front of this magician's feet and I remember…

HA! (this is so funny: what you remember, ya
know?)…

We're sittin' there at his feet and Hannah—she must've
been only six years old then—she looks at his hands,
turns to me like she's seen a ghost, and says… "don't
let him take my thumbs."

(She bursts out laughing.)

Which even then I remember…just…that just melted
my heart.

I put my arm around her and said: I won't. And she
just kinda curled up into me.

I wonder if she remembers that.

Hmm.

So it was weird to see this magician missin' a finger.

But he was a hack.

Still a great birthday though.

HANNAH: And so we're makin' this dinner, she's stirrin' the sauce, I'm poundin' the chicken in the sink…

SARAH: We're rememberin' all this stuff, makin' this dinner, and it's kinda fun. Ya know, it was kinda, I dunno, whatever, it was different, it was fun.

HANNAH: …and I see Sarah start to smile like she's *actually* smilin' like just this giant shit-eatin' grin on her face. And I was gonna make fun of her but I stopped myself.

SARAH: I can't remember the last time we had been together havin' that good 'a time.
It just made me wanna cry I was so…ya know, it sounds stupid, but it was just one 'a those times you feel so happy that you just wanna cry.
And those don't happen all that often.
You're lucky if you get two or three of those in your lifetime, and just…I dunno, whatever…I'm soundin' like a giant sissy here…

HANNAH: 'Fore you know it we're choppin' vegetables and we're stirrin' sauces and it's "do you remember when" and "what ever happened to so and so" and the Christmas with the sledding accident…
And we're laughin' and doublin' over and my cheeks, ya know that feelin' when your cheeks start to hurt 'cuz your laughin' and smilin' so much, and I can feel the corners of my mouth like they're strained like they're thin like they'll split open any minute and blood'll spill out and pour over my jaw and it'll be the first time I've ever had an injury that's hilarious.
And it's great.
And it's just, ya know, it's puttin' an ache in my stomach that hurts, I mean it really truly *hurts*, but it's that pain that makes you feel so full, like maybe that's how it once always was…

Like every waking minute used to be like this.
And not just for me, but that one time before we were
even here there was this fullness that consumed the
earth…
And somewhere down the line that fullness turned
empty and ravaged this place.
But that's how it was.
And that's I think the closest I've ever felt to my sister.
(*Beat*)
At least since we were little.

SARAH: I'm standin' there with the sauce and Hannah
can just *not stop* laughing.

HANNAH: I mean, I had just lost it.

SARAH: And I hear my Mom shout from the living
room: what's goin' on in there? You girls makin' fun of
me? Which made *me* go off…!

HANNAH: So then *Sarah* gets to laughin' where she's
snortin' like a warthog…!

SARAH: Which of course made it even worse!

HANNAH: And now we just can't stop, either of us!

SARAH: …we can't hardly contain ourselves, and then
all of a sudden…
(*A long pause*)
…I feel this wet tongue…lick my hand.

HANNAH: Vicky.

SARAH: (Fuckin'…Vicky.)

HANNAH: And Sarah…she yelped as loud as I ever
heard.

SARAH: It scared the hell outta' me.

HANNAH: It scared the shit outta' her…

SARAH: (I don't like bein' scared.)

HANNAH: …And Sarah, she leapt up in the air and her arm knocked the saucepan and tomato sauce just goes flyin' everywhere.

SARAH: Splatters all over the walls.

HANNAH: I mean everywhere…just the biggest mess you ever seen.

SARAH: The whole dinner's ruined.

HANNAH: Nobody's laughin' now. And Vicky…

SARAH: (All that work for nothin'.)

HANNAH: …Vicky starts lickin' up the tomato sauce off the floor.
Like: all is well. Like: whatever.
And that's when I looked up…and I saw Sarah…just starin' at her.
Starin' at this sheep.
And everything slowed down.
And I could see in her eyes what she was thinkin'.
And Sarah turns to me and says: grab her.
Without a second thought I grabbed two fists of Vicky's wool and dragged her over to me like I was the goddamn Marlboro man, like I'd done this before but I hadn't ever.
She tried to squirm away but I put her between my legs and straddled her and squeezed her torso with my thighs.
And Sarah…comes up to Vicky and swats her across the nose with her hand.
Ya know, like: "bad sheep."
And it makes sense or whatever.
It's normal.
But then I can see, like…I can see this…
I see this little somethin' in her just…click over.
And it made me click over too.

Sarah just stands there for a second.
Lookin' into Vicky's eyes, into these sheep eyes.
Just real calm.
And she looks over onto the counter...
And on the counter was the meat tenderizer...
(Beat)
"No fuckin' way." "Yes." But, "No fuckin' way."
(Beat)

SARAH: I looked at that sheep. And that thing...it had
no idea what was goin' on.
I mean...it was just oblivious.
Well...I grabbed...the meat tenderizer...
And I swung it down over her head.
And Vicky looked up at me and kinda blinked a few
times and then it was almost like she sneezed—like the
damn thing knocked a cold out of her or somethin'—
and then she shook her head and stared at me again
like it never happened.
Like she was totally...unfazed.
And it just kinda made me mad.
It made me mad that it didn't do anything to her.
So I did it again.
(Beat)
And then I did it again.
(Pause)
And then I didn't stop.
(Beat)

HANNAH: It's weird, but there was not a part 'a me that
wanted to stop her.
She took that meat tenderizer and just went to town on
Vicky and...it just gave me a thrill.
And as she was swingin' I squeezed Vicky tighter and
tighter with my thighs and I could feel her lungs press
up against me...

And it seemed like Vicky was just made 'a steel or somethin' 'cuz she just wasn't reactin', like it didn't faze her one bit…

It was so weird 'cuz I could hear Entertainment Tonight blarin' in the background and I knew my Mom couldn't hear us over the T V and the theme song is goin' and as Sarah was swingin' I noticed that she was in perfect rhythm with the theme song…

So there was just like this crazy fuckin' perfection in this moment, like it was all happenin' together, like in sync, ya know, like it was supposed to happen, and it just took me to this place that made my feet feel heavy, like it was the opposite of feelin' drunk but ten times more…

And the theme song stops.

And Sarah stops.

And she's breathin' heavy.

And I look into her eyes…

And I seen Sarah grab Vicky by her snout. And she started sayin' somethin' to her.

I don't know what, but she just started talkin' to it through her teeth in kind of a whisper.

And all 'a sudden she takes that meat pounder… And she kinda winds up…and she swings it…one more time right across Vicky's mouth.

And this time…umm…somethin' happened.

(Beat. She opens her mouth to talk but can't.)

It was somethin' worse than before because this time when she swung it across her face I felt somethin' wet and heavy hit my arm.

And I wasn't sure if it was spit or blood or somethin' else…

But umm…Vicky…I felt her kinda go limp between my legs…

And I let her go…and she sort of stumbles forward but she's still standin' up…but I can only see the back of her.

And she's standin'…and she runs…straight into the kitchen cupboards.

And then she does it again.

And I'm thinkin'…ya know: what the hell she tryin' to do?

But then Vicky turns around…

And she looks at us…

And I about shit my pants.

SARAH: Her cheek…had been sliced open a little…and her lips were kinda pushed to one side.

And you could see all of her teeth. Like they're fully exposed and they shouldn't be.

And so it looked like she was smiling, ya know?

HANNAH: Looked happy as a goddamn clam.

SARAH: And her eyes were open real wide, much wider than usual, and her tongue, her tongue was like hangin' out and she was panting and she had this giant smile on her face but it wasn't a smile it was just the shape her face took after I hit her…

HANNAH: She's panting with this big old smile, her tongue's out, and it's like her whole face is lifted back and she's just starin' at me with these big old baleful eyes, just a fuckin' tractor beam right into my soul, and I'm thinkin' we retarded the sheep!

SARAH: We mentally damaged this damn sheep and it'll never be the same and we're in deep shit and that's what I'm thinkin'!

HANNAH: And I can't wrap my damn head around this.

SARAH: I mean I'm lookin' at this sheep and it's like it just happened so fast!

HANNAH: Here this thing is one minute, normal as can be in our kitchen and the next minute—boom—we've just turned its brains into fuckin' soup. Ya know?!
So it's like: what'd we do here?

SARAH: It just shouldn't have been happy and I'm thinkin'…

HANNAH: What on earth did we do here?

SARAH: …I'm thinkin', ya know…

HANNAH: What the hell do you say, there's nothin' to say…

SARAH: …I'm thinkin': how'd I do that?
How could I have done that?
How am I gonna explain this…?

HANNAH: What do you do with a retarded sheep?

SARAH: Mom's in the next room.

HANNAH: She didn't hear it. I don't think she heard it.

SARAH: I hear her turn off the T V.

(Beat)

HANNAH: Shit. Maybe she heard it.

SARAH: And it was quiet and no one's sayin' anything and I can tell that she's listenin' from the other room like she heard somethin'.
(Beat. She awaits the break of silence.)
Hannah says:

HANNAH: You alright in there Mom?
She asked me what was goin' on and I said: oh nothin', we just had a spill…I spilled the sauce…
And she waits for a second like she thinks somethin's up.
I hear the T V go back on.
Sarah and I look at each other.

SARAH: Here was this mess of a kitchen and Vicky, her snout all brown and red, and this crooked grin across her face.

HANNAH: The tomato sauce was everywhere so it just looked like a slaughterhouse gone nuts.

SARAH: I grabbed Vicky by the neck and took her out to the stables and had Hannah wipe up the mess.

HANNAH: Then we finished makin' dinner and ate around the table and it was the most awkward fuckin' meal I have ever had in my life.

SARAH: Mom started askin' questions but then stopped when I brought out her birthday cake.
I noticed there was a little sauce that had splattered on it, which was annoying.

HANNAH: We sang her Happy Birthday and then Sarah asked if I would put her to bed, so I did.
I laid her down.
And I don't usually do this but for some reason, before I left the room…I kissed her on the head, and said: happy birthday Mom. Told her I loved her.
I think it surprised her.
'Cuz she got quiet.
And she didn't move.
She got really quiet.

SARAH: Then me and Hannah got to work.
(She takes a hair tie from her pocket and puts her hair up into a ponytail.)
We weren't about to give her back to Mom in that shape…

HANNAH: She's too far gone.

SARAH: Mom'd flip.

HANNAH: And I didn't want that thing around. Fuckin' retarded sheep haunting my dreams? No way.

SARAH: There's a couple things you could do at this point…
First off you could just try and let it loose. Let it run away.
But the problem with that is the damn thing is tagged and the other ranchers in town'll return it soon's it shows up.

HANNAH: Besides, with the state of its brain, I think it'd just run around in circles until it got tired.

SARAH: Your second option is you could bury it.

HANNAH: I didn't wanna bury it…

SARAH: Neither of us wanted to bury it.

HANNAH: 'Cuz if you bury it you gotta kill it first and I didn't wanna kill it.

SARAH: Hannah just couldn't.

HANNAH: I really didn't wanna kill it.

SARAH: And neither of us knew the easiest way.
 'Cuz if you kill it then you got blood and you still gotta bury it. And even then you're not really *finished* with it.

HANNAH: A buried sheep is still a sheep, which we wanted nothin' to do with.

SARAH: Besides…it's against the law to bury a sheep in Colorado for reasons of disease and all that.

Don't ask me how I know that…

HANNAH: I just hated the idea of it…

SARAH: …I love the law.
(She goes up to the newspapers and takes out a knife from her back pocket and opens the knife and cuts the remaining twine that binds the papers. She takes the twine off the papers and tosses it away.)

HANNAH: I didn't even wanna think about it.
Butcherin' it, I mean.

(Beat. Timidly:)

Once when I was a kid we were at a petting zoo
and I accidentally stepped on a baby chick but it
didn't totally die and I was afraid I'd get in trouble
if somebody found it just squirmin' around there
so I stepped on it again until it was dead and I got
some blood on my shoe and then I just threw it away
somewhere, and ever since then I didn't like the idea of
killin'.

(Beat)

I'm sorry. I didn't mean that to sound cruel.

It was an accident.

I'm not all that bad.

Or maybe I am, I dunno.

(Yeah...I prolly am.)

SARAH: (Coming back downstage) So, couldn't let it loose.
Couldn't slaughter it. Couldn't bury it.

(She stops.)

Only one option left.

(Pause)

HANNAH: (You gotta burn that shit.)

SARAH: That's the only way.

HANNAH: That's the only way we're gonna be done
with it, ya know? If we wanna be free 'a this mess we
got to cast that fucker into the fire and incinerate the
damn thing.

SARAH: So we agree. That's what we're doin'.

HANNAH: There's a place out behind the stables that
we can do it. Nice clean patch 'a dirt kinda tucked
away so no one can see it.

It was gettin' pretty late and there's a nice stretch 'a prairie between our house and the next about a quarter mile away, so if we were gonna do it, now was the time.

SARAH: I tell Hannah to go collect some tinder and some wood and I'll go get Vicky…

HANNAH: I went and got some newspaper and some wood from the side 'a the house. Started preppin' this fire.
(She starts to bring a few logs from the side of the stage to upstage center where the ash lies. She arranges the logs along with some of the kindling and newspaper in the center of the circle of ash.)

(As SARAH speaks, HANNAH begins to position the materials, preparing a pyre.)

(We see HANNAH's shadow loom large and heavy as she works, the girls' memories coming to life.)

SARAH: I went up to Vicky's stall and saw her body dimly lit by the moon.
God. She still had that look on her face with the teeth and the smile and everything. Just horrifying.
I couldn't bear to look at her long and I just wanted all this to be over quick so I picked her up into my arms and walked out across our property to where Hannah was makin' the fire.

(HANNAH wipes her hands on her jeans, cleaning them of ash and dirt, then goes and grabs a bottle of lighter fluid.)

SARAH: I dragged that sheep out and the light of the moon weighed on my shoulders as my shadow big in front of me bounced in a weird way like it looked as if I wasn't alone but that there was a stranger leading me deeper into that dark prairie, gettin' away from that bright moon.

As I was walkin' with that heap of wool and skin and
organs I could feel it's blood circulatin'.

It was warm and I could feel its veins pump, like a
hose that hadn't been turned on since summer before.

And my shadow in front of me looked like some
monster come alive from the ground that walked with
this bumbling rhythm. Like it wasn't me.

HANNAH: I was buildin' that fire in the dark and it
kinda spooked me, ya know.

All those ghost stories you remember from when you
were a kid start to come back somehow when you're
outside alone at night.

I put the logs together and I was sweatin' and it felt
like I was doin' some ancient task.

Like: who used to do this? Like: where did I learn this?

I've learned this but I don't remember learnin' this.

But I sort of knew it.

And I felt like there was some step I was missin'.

SARAH: The moon stayed bright for another few
minutes but then I saw my shadow disappear as a
cloud rolled in front of it an' made the ground dark as
pitch out there.

So dark I didn't know what I was walkin' on.

Like I couldn't trust the ground beneath my feet.

I don't think I've ever seen the moon go away that
quick.

Seemed like it figured out what I was fixin' to do and
decided to shield its eyes from the mess of it all.

I don't blame it.

HANNAH: I had got some lighter fluid from the garage
and sprayed it all over the logs.

Made sure that thing'd light up quick and hot.

SARAH: I found Hannah behind the stables and tossed
Vicky to the ground and wrapped up her legs real
quick with this twine I grabbed from her stall.
Felt sorta' like my Dad, wranglin' that thing, 'cept I
wasn't nearly as good.

HANNAH: I was sorta' tremblin' and I would never say
this to Sarah but I kinda cried for a quick second.
But it was dark so I don't think she saw me.
I don't know where she got the strength but Sarah
was tyin' her up like it was just another chore she was
doin', like it was just second-nature, and she asked me
for the lighter fluid and soaked Vicky's wool with it.

SARAH: I picked her up and laid her down in the center
'a those logs…

HANNAH: We both stood back for a second and
watched Vicky as she laid there. Smilin'.

SARAH: *(Painfully)* I thought of my Dad.
Then I thought of my Mom.

HANNAH: I lit the match and tossed it in there.
It lit up with a whoosh so quick it singed the hair on
my arms.
Vicky caught fire immediately.

SARAH: The fire goes up. Bigger than I thought it'd
be…and you know…we figured the flames would just,
ya know, automatically engulf her.

HANNAH: Like it'd just happen…

SARAH: Vicky was already screwed up in the head, we
figured she'd just accept her fate and…give in.
Well she's in there. And she's burnin' pretty good.
But she starts makin' this sound.

HANNAH: It's like she sort of screams and bleats and
honks all at the same time.

SARAH: Almost sounds like she's sayin' somethin'. Or like she's tryin' to say somethin'. Tryin' her hardest to communicate with those that are killin' it.

HANNAH: And it was very human...ya know? Like it was talkin' to me. Cryin' for help.

SARAH: Thing's hollerin'. And we're just mesmerized. You know, like the same as when you look into a campfire: There's just somethin' clean about it.
There was part of me wanted to put my hand in there. I wouldn't do it of course, but there's part of me wanted to feel that fire.
Toss myself into those flames.

HANNAH: And so it's hollerin' but there's nothin' we could do...and we start to notice that's it's takin' a while, ya know, for Vicky to die.

SARAH: Like way longer than we thought.

HANNAH: And I look over at Sarah and I say, ya know, "This is not good." An' she's like: "Yeah, no shit."

SARAH: And so the thing starts squirmin' around. Like it realized its noises wouldn't do anything and so now it's gonna try and get outta' there.
And we didn't even think that could even happen, ya know, because those flames, ya know...we thought that fire was hot enough to just...
So it's flailin' around in there.
An' I'm thinkin' well shit, I tied the thing up...

HANNAH: Maybe we didn't tie it tight enough...

SARAH: ...I just did it real quick, ya know, but maybe I shoulda' thought to tie it better.
But it's only so much thinkin' you can do when you've got the idea in your head that the best choice you could make would be to incinerate a piece 'a livestock.

HANNAH: So we see it in there and it's goin' off. It's shiftin' the logs around. It's just strugglin'.
And I mean it's sufferin' like you wouldn't believe.
But it's strange, ya know...it was like the flames, they weren't doin' anything to her.
All its coat was on fire but her head was still ok.

SARAH: She was on fire...but she wasn't burning.

HANNAH: She wasn't changed. She was only sufferin'.

SARAH: And it's this ball of flames just tossin' around in there and it starts to move a hell of a lot and I'm thinkin': shit...she's gonna try and get outta' that fire.

HANNAH: She's tryin' to get outta' the fire...

SARAH: And I see her squirm outta' the ropes...

HANNAH: ...and her coat is just blazin'...

SARAH: Her body is totally engulfed in flames...

HANNAH: And she rolls over...

SARAH: And sure enough...she hops up out of the fire...!

HANNAH: This ball 'a flames...

SARAH: And she takes off...!

HANNAH: The fucker just darts outta' there...!

SARAH: Just b-lines it out onto the plains...

HANNAH: Out into the dark...

SARAH: Quicker than a jackrabbit...

HANNAH: And we see this orange blaze take off into the night...

SARAH: And I'm in shock and what do we do...

HANNAH: And I turn to Sarah...

SARAH: This is how it starts...

HANNAH: I'm lookin' at my sister...

SARAH: This is how people's lives end...

HANNAH: What do we do?

SARAH: This is how you catch the whole damn state on fire...

HANNAH: What do we do?

SARAH: We're gonna start a brush fire the size of Weld County and I'm gonna pay for it.

HANNAH: What are we gonna do?!
And Sarah goes:

(Beat)

SARAH: O K.

HANNAH: And she takes off after Vicky...

SARAH: But she's runnin' so fast...

HANNAH: You'd never think a sheep'd be that speedy but I guess when you're on fire...

SARAH: This ball of flames just gets smaller and smaller and then I can barely see her...

HANNAH: But Sarah's just bookin' it out across the plains.

SARAH: And then she disappears.
I figured she just went over some ridge, out 'a sight or somethin'.
So I run out towards her...must've been a good minute by this point.
And I'm runnin' and I realize: what the hell am I gonna do if I catch her?
There's nothin' I *can* do, it's just whatever happens is gonna happen no matter if I find her or not but I ran and it felt right to run it's just somethin' to do...
So I stopped. And I sat.
And I felt like I'd been out there before in that dark.

Like right to that exact place. Like I'd done this before, like there was something...familiar about it.

(*Covered in the shadows far upstage,* HANNAH *brings on more wood and arranges it on the pyre.*)

SARAH: There was somethin' I recognized about that ground.
I thought maybe I was just rememberin' somethin' from when I was a kid or maybe...I dunno, but I coulda' swore I done this before.
It's like I was out there and I felt there was somethin' from my family that I never learned but I know.

(HANNAH *tosses a log off. It lands with a thud.*)

SARAH: And that scared me when I thought about that.

(HANNAH *tosses off another log. Thud*)

SARAH: But God...I coulda' swore I done that before.

(*Another log. Thud*)

SARAH: And I just wanted to die.
I stared out into the dark night, lookin' for that light, and when I closed my eyes it was no different and so I opened 'em again but I saw nothin'.
And I saw nothin' for a long time.

(*Pause*)

Until I saw Vicky.

HANNAH: Sarah's off runnin' like a madman and I'm thinkin': well what the hell does she intend to do?
We've got a animal ablaze out on the plains.
We're lookin' at a Colorado inferno here if we don't keep our heads on straight.
So I head back towards the house.
I bring some water back down to the fire and put it out and then I go to the garage.

Decide I'll hop in my car with some buckets of
water and maybe drive out, see if I can spot her and
extinguish this whole mess 'fore it puts me in prison.
I open the garage, just prayin' that all this hasn't woke
Mom, and I remembered that my Dad used to store
water jugs in the bed of his truck. He used to use 'em
to water the sheep when they were out to pasture.
(Beat)
So I remember this and umm…I take the…cover…I
take the cover off Dad's truck and there was that smell
that reminded me…
(Pause)
And I climbed into the bed of the truck…and umm…
I'm sorry…
(Pause)
(Desperately holding back tears:)
I'm sorry, I'm just…I'm tryin' to keep it together here…
(Beat)
It's just that I miss him very much.
(Beat)
So anyway…I'm in the back of his truck…and I…laid
down.
I laid down in the back 'a Dad's truck.
And I fell asleep.
I don't know how but I fell right the fuck asleep.

SARAH: In that kinda dark you can't miss even the
smallest bit of light.
Gets to a point where you feel like your senses are
goin' funny on ya…but it's just nothin'.
So I'm out there…and you're never gonna believe it…
But far off in the distance…I seen a blaze like an orange
comet stream across the horizon.
I got up and ran towards her.
I chased her for a ways but then I seen her stumble and
fall…

But I didn't know why she fell…
So I caught up to her…
And as I approached her I could see through the
flames…somethin' movin' or burnin' or I dunno…
And so I thought: well shit, she's finally burnin'.
But then she starts bleatin', makin' that noise she was
makin' before.
And she starts…gnashin' her teeth for some reason,
like grindin' 'em…
And I see her stomach sort of shift around, like there's
a snake inside it or somethin'.
Just the weirdest lookin' thing…like she's gonna burst.
And it's turned with its back to me, ya know…and I
uhh…I see this…
(Beat)
(Shit… Can't believe I'm sayin' this.) It's just….
(Pause. She collects herself and continues.)
I seen her backside… start to open up.
Start to just spread open.
And I could barely see it but there was this…
(Goddammit.)
I see this row of teeth…come out the back of it.
An' then I seen a snout.
An' this whole…head just emergin' out from it.
It won't take me goin' further for you to get what I'm
about to say…but the lamb I seen come from her was
the worst thing I ever seen in my life.
How, I have no idea…but there it was…layin' there
like it was waitin' for some different world, all free and
open.
It lay there and Vicky looked at it. And then looked at
me.
And then she ran away into the night, with her wool
still blazin'.
I couldn't help but go up to it.

After Vicky ran away it was so dark and I couldn't find it right away…so I felt for it on the ground and I found it and I laid my hands on it.

And I was hopin'…I dunno, I was thinkin' maybe it coulda' still been alive even though it didn't look it and I felt around on it to see if I could find a pulse…

But I didn't.

And I knew that was probably my fault.

I wanted… (this is just gonna sound so lame) but ya know I wanted it to see somethin' green.

Just for a second…ya know? Just a place that seemed lush, grassy…

But instead it's brought into this dark black of a night…where some thin wind fans the flames of my big fuckin' mistakes out across the plains of this god-forsaken place.

Just a little green…how it was supposed to be.

I wiped it off with my shirt and picked it up.

I couldn't stand to have it layin' there, chewed up by the coyotes or just…whatever: freezin'.

I headed back towards the house.

(She goes upstage to the pyre and stuffs it with tinder before spraying it with lighter fluid.)

HANNAH: I slept in the back 'a that truck for I don't know how long…

I woke up and I forgot where I was until I didn't.

I stared out across the black prairie from the garage, picturing Sarah out there lookin' around. I wondered where she was.

SARAH: I thought about Vicky, where she was. I could see her in my mind: the flame of her body tracin' across the plains.

Tauntin' me. Just to spite me.

HANNAH: I got outta' the bed of the truck, and I went inside the house.

SARAH: I was carryin' that lamb back home…

HANNAH: But when I got inside…

SARAH: I knew we'd have to do away with it.

HANNAH: …I could hardly believe it…

SARAH: We'd have to get rid of it.

HANNAH: It just scared me so bad…

SARAH: There's no other choice.

HANNAH: 'Cuz when I walked in the house… Standin' right there by the window…was my Mom.

(The shadow of a robed woman appears far upstage; a glimpse of HANNAH's *memory come to life. Pause)*

HANNAH: And she was…standing there…she was standing right there looking right at me.
And I could tell, ya know…she was waiting for me.
And I thought…well this is it. She's seen the whole thing.
There's no way outta' this.
What's done can't be undone.
And I just…I didn't know what to say.
Her eyes…her eyes looked soft and sunk like she was about to cry…
We stood there in that dark house as the white of her robe shone bright like something against nothing and my eyes began to see more of her.
The shadow on her face made her look somehow different, in a way I'd never seen before. But it was the *right* way… (ya know?)
I wanted to tell her…to tell her I was sorry.
That I was so sorry.
But before I could…I saw her mouth…start to tighten up…
And slowly…she began to smile.
Like a real, true, happy smile.

And it reminded me...ya know, it was like the same smile I remember seein' when my Dad gave her Vicky.
And I realized...that she didn't know.
She didn't know what we had done.
And as she smiled, she looked at me and said:
'I just wanted to thank you for a wonderful birthday.'
And she reached out...and handed me these:
(She reaches into her pocket and takes out the keys to her father's truck. She holds them out. Pause. The keys rattle as her hand shakes.)
I wrapped my arms around her and started to cry...but she thought it was for some better reason.
I felt the shortness of her breath as her lungs pressed up against me.
I had it in me...to...I had it in me to just...click over.
To just...squeeze her tighter...and tighter.
But I didn't.
'Cuz with her face against mine she whispered: 'He always wanted you to have it.'
(Pause. She closes her eyes.)

(The shadow of the robed woman disappears.)

HANNAH: I heard her say that a million times in my head...
Until I heard somethin' else:

SARAH: *(Far upstage, softly, from the dark)* Hannah... Hannah.

(HANNAH opens her eyes.)

HANNAH: It was a faint voice out in the distance.
I stared out across that black ground to see what it was but it felt like my eyes had never opened.
Like I was lost in some awful rest.
And I hoped that was the case.
Even here...

Even now…
(To the heavens, bashfully:)
(Right?)
From the darkness I heard a woman's voice cry out to me saying:

SARAH: Hannah… Where are you…?

HANNAH: I went to the window and turned on the porch light.
I looked out…and I saw a figure far across that dark prairie.

(SARAH is illuminated, revealed to be carrying something heavy in her arms, covered in a garbage bag.)

HANNAH: It was a person, carryin' somethin'.
It rocked from side to side with some determined rhythm.
Like it was set out to do somethin'.

(SARAH places the garbage bag on top of the pyre.)

HANNAH: And it was the face of my sister began to take shape as she stumbled towards our house.
But I couldn't see what was she was carryin'.
She kept calling me.

SARAH: Can you hear me?
(She slowly takes a book of matches out of her pocket.)

HANNAH: But I wasn't sure what she wanted me to do.
Cuz she was so far out there…
She was so distant…
That I barely recognized her.
But it was Sarah.
It was my sister.
Set out…with somethin' in her arms.

(SARAH *strikes a match 3 times before it lights. She stares at it, burning in her hand, then extends her arm and holds the flame above the pyre.*)

HANNAH: And she seemed so far away.

(*The flame continues to burn. Pause*)

(*Blackout*)

(*Music*)

END OF PLAY

www.ingramcontent.com/pod-product-compliance
Lightning Source LLC
Chambersburg PA
CBHW070030110426
42741CB00035B/2710